Marjorie Saiser

Lost in Seward County

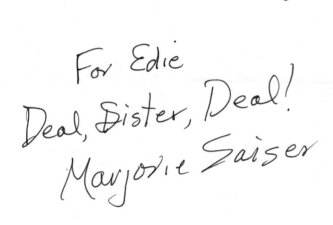

For Edie
Deal, ~~Sister~~, Deal!
Marjorie Saiser

The Backwaters Press

Also by Marjorie Saiser

Bones of a Very Fine Hand, The Backwaters Press, 1999

Some of these poems first appeared in *Poets On, Zone 3, Blue Hotel, Meridian, Credo, Plains Song Review, Nebraska Poets Calendar*, and *PlainSense*.

"Washing My Hair in the Platte" and "Lying on the Driveway Studying Stars" were first published in *Prairie Schooner*, and are reprinted by permission of University of Nebraska Press.

First Printing, 1000 copies, October, 2001.

Published by: The Backwaters Press
                 Greg Kosmicki, Editor/Publisher
                 3502 North 52nd Street
                 Omaha, Nebraska 68104-3506
                 (402) 451-4052
                 GKosm62735@AOL.com
                 www.thebackwaterspress.homestead.com

ISBN : 0-9677149-5-8

Printed in the United States by:
Morris Publishing
3212 East Highway 30
Kearney, NE 68847
1-800-650-7888

Lost in Seward County

Marjorie Saiser

Many thanks to these supporters of The Backwaters Press without whose generous contributions and subscriptions the publication of this book would not have been possible.

ANGELS

Steve and Kathy Kloch
Greg and Barb Kuzma
Rich and Eileen Zochol

BENEFACTORS

Barbara Schmitz

PATRONS

Guy and Jennie Duncan
Cheryl Kessell
Maureen Toberer
Frederick Zydek

SPONSORS

Paul and Mildred Kosmicki
Gary Leisman and Wendy Adams
Jeff and Patty Knag
Matt Mason
Pat Murray and Jeanne Schuler
Carol Schmid
Alan and Kim Stoler
Don Taylor

FRIENDS

J.V. Brummels
Twyla Hansen
Tim O'Connor
Jim and Mary Pipher

For Don

Lost in Seward County

To Whirl in that Column

The View Aloft   1
Night Flight   3
From This Angle   4
To the Man in First Class Who Will Not
Look at Me Today   5
There Are No Atheists in Airplanes   7
Re-entry   9
Looking For Ted   10
St. Cecilia, Seward County   13
Taking the Baby to the Prairie   15
Nine-Mile Prairie, April   16
Not So Much Bottom Line as Bluestem   18
The African American Quilt Exhibit   21
The Living, the Warm   23

The Gold Ring of its Eye

What My Life Is   29
The White Lamb in the Yard   33
The Muse is a Little Girl   34
Often He Came to Pick Up His Wife   35
Teaching Me to Write   36
What She Taught Me   38
Dear Writing,   39
The Light that Makes the Web Show Up   41

What the Moon Wants   44
We'll Drive the Olds   45
I Don't Want to Speak Car   46
In No Hurry   47
While I Sleep   49
Father   50
Otto   52
At the Derby Star   54
A Man in Love With Wind   55
Frying Eggs in Bacon Fat   56
The Saucepan, Washed   57
Losing   58

Hawk Over Snow

Washing My Hair in the Platte   63
Videotaping the Total Lunar Eclipse   64
This Ain't No Bass Boat Day   66
The Caffeine Kicks In   68
The Cleaning Wind   69
Prairie Pretends to be Mild   71
Holed Up In Valentine, Nebraska   72
Yes, These Are My People   73
Thinking of Emily Dickinson   74
There Are Poems in Every Tree   75
Lying on the Driveway, Studying Stars   76
To Leave My Grandma   77
No Greenhouse Flowers For Your Grave   78
Summer, Striking   79
You Gave Me A Typewriter   81
As Long As Someone Remembers   82
You Know My Father Prayed for You   83
Lying Up Against My Husband In the Dark   84
My Old Aunts Play Canasta in a Snowstorm   85

Lost in Seward County

Marjorie Saiser

To Whirl in that Column

The View Aloft

There's a dusting of snow, a white edge
along each side of that doubling-back
string that may be a road through the mountains.
I know mountains, I recognize them
from 33,000 feet, I know tree cover, but I can't tell
deciduous or conifer. Too high for that kind
of resolution. I know *town*: pieces scattered

like bits of stone. There's an eel that may be
a river, one leg splaying out from his body.
He's gone, passed below us.
There's a lake on the side of a mountain.
It's that flat jade stone laid up against
the straight line of the dam.

Look what we've made,
what we've done with our material.
We could do better—I intend to—
but still there's something good
about how we've dug into the crust
as if we wanted to stay. It's home;

we connect our cities like rooms.
We circle what we can't do without:
the *fleur de lis* bodies of water.
We draw our matrixes: this street,
this crooked road crossing this other.
This road follows a river as far as it can.
There's a port fanning its piers, its fingers,
into the water. I can't see what we've done
at the edges. It fogs out; it's too far to see.

The view nobody has is my face at this window,
this window one eye in the eyes that line

the side of the ship. My eye, me.

Liking the variegated view, liking the light
and the height and the distance,
liking the fact that I don't yet know
the planet inside, slowly rolling,
don't yet know what's turning in me.
Revolving, about to come into view.

Night Flight

From 18F I see only the wing,
see only metal and rivets and painted black arrows
and partially worn-off letters saying things like NO STEP.
From 18F, or anywhere on this plane,
I could see, if I want to, the video.
I could, evidently, watch ads for Buzz Lightyear, the series.
But I am watching *us*, the community
of 1090 to Denver. We are facing forward
as though in a tunnel or tube,
dots of light in a row above our heads.
We are ranks of readers, sleepers,

or we are the cast of *Our Town*;
we are cast as the dear departed,
sitting onstage on our chairs—supposed to be graves—
looking straight ahead, talking among ourselves,
never looking at Emily, the living,
when she comes to visit the cemetery.
We are not turning toward Emily;

we are numbers and letters facing forward.
From 18F I see we are regular in our posture,
regular in our habits.

In my row we are raising similar cups from similar trays,
oddly comforting:
now this head, now that one, lowers to drink.
One by one we sip our mutual nectar;
one by one we set it down.

From This Angle

It's a small plane from L.A. to Palm Springs.
Reminds me of a Ford my father had:
when the engine purred, it roared.

The propeller, like all swiftly moving things,
blurs and becomes invisible,
leaves only the engine casing
and the Pacific,
the Pacific because, though we are going inland,
we, like an old Ford, go the other way first,
and make a long jog back.
Hello, Ocean. Bluegreen. Primeval.
To die in water would be a death indeed.

The engine reaches out
beyond the wing like an eagle's head.
The nose of the propeller, from this angle,
has the shape of an eagle's beak,
and beyond it, and under it, as we bank left,

the water,
jewel blue, perfect.
How human to conjecture an eagle,
and to ride it, searching, over the ocean.
I fabricate it from ordinary transportation,
ride it as if toward an abiding home,

huge and deep,
when I have played,
and played out,
and come to the end of—not yet, not yet—
my swiftly-moving, eagle-wing days.

To the Man in First Class Who Will Not
Look at Me Today

We come on, the general boarders,
we file by and our line slows and I am
the end of it, in the aisle of the first class compartment,
waiting, one hand behind me for the handle of the bag with wheels,
one hand in front with my carry-on. You,

having no particular place to focus
and having finished or forgotten your copy of whatever you read,
look briefly at my sweater, my red beads.
Briefly briefly past my face face face.
I catch on fast. I look out your window to the tarmac, to the
four-wheeled sideless topless vehicle with orange cones
piled on it. I focus on its faded triangular flag
flapping like a tongue. The steward

begins his spiel into his microphone:
overhead and *baggage* and *compartment* and *stow,*
and I am the end of the line, I can't move
forward, can't pass your steel-wool chest hair
at the neck of your unbottoned shirt,
your thick gold chain

and I am sweating, waiting,
my too-much baggage like an anchor in the aisle.
I have dragged it through the airport,
airline to airline, my original flight last-minute cancelled.

Hey, first class
Hey, gold chain
I am 4D, the rows they call last

I am sweaty, I made it this far, I made it—
my black turtleneck reeking,

my hands full—I blow the hair out of my right eye.

Hey, leg room
Hey, ice cubes
Live a little.
Relax.

There Are No Atheists in Airplanes

There are no atheists in airplanes, or very few,
or at least not in prop jobbies, at least not in
turbulence, at least not in rain over the Gulf.
It's what we have, 12,000 feet, cloud nosing
up to the windows, and potholes in the road.
We're in this together, the guy behind me says.
He says *Does it cost extra to fly*

antique? I'm glad he's here, our high priest,
wise-cracking behind me right from the first.
Right from the first, when the captain in his blue
uniform, three stripes on the forearm, cannot get the door

to the cockpit open. His blue back to his passengers,
the captain jiggles the lock. The captain, turning his key in the lock
and getting nowhere. Behind me the high priest says,
I think this guy and I were at the same party.

He raises his wonderful voice and he says
*Your key's upside down and you're not
holding your mouth right.* When we're idling on the tarmac,
the plane rolls backwards. Behind me, he says, *Oh well,
I didn't want to leave anyway.*

He speaks for all of us, doesn't he,
the woman in the seat ahead who has had
somebody spray her hair orange
and green, with blue dots the size of hives
running up the french roll from nape to crest.

The man beside me who takes off his glasses
to read a page titled *Vanguard and the New Funds.*
The tall fellow ahead of him, his head
tilted down as if in prayer, the lines on the skin
of his neck like a map of tributaries. We hit

a particularly large hole in the road;
the guy behind me says *What's a long life*
anyway? It's what we have, this voice
over the shoulder. I can't see him
now, but I saw him after boarding when I turned
to sink into my seat. His hair is an even quarter-inch

all over, dome and sides. His sunglasses wrap around;
on a Star Trek set, he could send and receive
from almost any galaxy. He's what I have.
What I'm going to is a welcome home,
a drop-the-bags use-both-hands kind,
lift-me-off-the-ground kissing.
For now it's a prop jobbie,

it's turbulence. But here's a change: blue sky
in the top third of the window,
as if a bell, ringing. Behind me, the high priest
says, *It's about time.* Here's the stewardess
in the aisle, trundling her cart along as if it
were our communion rail.

Re-entry

Those squares of white are snow. Those squares mean
section lines. I'm almost home, that part of the world
where grids make very secure corners for you,
where miles behave themselves in straight lines,
no cock-eyed catty-corner tricks. Everything is

north-and-south, or east-and-west, circumspect.
I know the people who have been tracking through
that snow. I know their temper, their temperature,
the way they get through whatever happens:
Blizzard: scoop it. Drought: quit your whining.
Bad luck: So?

I love you, you snow and drought
and tornado people. I know how you'll bat
down confidence, call it "the big head,"
how you don't have time for me. I tell you,
you big-hearted grid-crazies, I came from you.

I came out of your loins on a cold day after work.
I have your genes, your no-fooling DNA. I'm no
hot-house bloom. I'm going to root deep like bur oak,
like downy gentian, for the duration.
I'm going to jump out of my banks

every spring thaw. I'll be a red bird on white
snow, a mustang on free range. I'm a rabbit
and the wolf, too. Tornado, cyclone, chinook,
thunder-boomer. I will dance
in your every snowbank.

Looking For Ted

I am lost in Seward County, looking for Ted,
for his house, his front door near a prairie, near a barn.
I am far from settling into the chair at his table, far
from his old dogs, Hattie and Bud; they do not
revolve about me, slow wobbly satellites on his
hardwood kitchen floor. I am lost, asking
directions in the general store in Malcolm, lost

near a cardtable in the corner where the clerk
plays pitch, sucks on her cigarette, and she
cannot tell me how to get to Ted's, cannot
help me, sorry. But the man at her left, dealing, says
you can't miss it, follow the road. He gestures in a
direction, and I am dismissed like so much smoke.

I do indeed follow the road and I do what I
can't do—miss it—but it is a fine day to be lost,
the air soft as spring, the water dripping
off the eaves of the farmhouse where I pull in
for further directions, the snow sagging, the soil
warming and softening, softening too much
because now I am stuck in the yard,

nobody home, nobody looking through the blinds
to see who is stuck, an overweight male beagle
the only creature available to bark. No matter.
I laugh, lost, stuck, the air coming in the window
so springlike, Ted waiting so Ted-like, his dogs
hoping for whatever it is that Ted is cooking and
stirring. I am stuck, the beagle repeats himself,
the farmwife stays away, I shift into reverse.
My worthless car does not comply, its treadless
treasonous tires spinning—until a tiny subsoil
miracle, a patch less soggy—

my great little car rises on that less soggy island,
it rolls, chugs goodbye to all beagles, it navigates,
sails up the drive, up the soft snowy lane, reaches
its miserable apogee, remembers then it is a small

underpaid car, refuses the last twelve feet,
declines to nose nearer the top of the lane, which
refusal pre-empts my turning either right or left,
right or left being my choices at the top if I could
reach them, if I were not sufficiently lost so that
right or left is no big deal. The sun shines
springlike, and the hills near Garland or Malcolm,
whichever, roll toward any convenient horizon.
Hattie and Buddy give up on the soup kettle and
draw a bead on the loaf of bread Ted is sawing into,
that *I* would be sawing into,
were I not motionless at the apex
of a small rise, trying to get out of a farmyard
onto a road in Seward County, or at least in Nebraska,
none of which would look familiar even if I could
get my car up there to look around. I get out to
survey. The beagle at the bottom does a horse laugh;
I study the sky for a sign. I slam the door, Ted
checks his watch and stirs the split pea, wonders
if he has added the carrots too soon. I am far from
dining, far from cup and plate and kiwi. Therefore I gun it.
My marvelous car—sweet little bright dependable genius—
burps to the top, to the lip of the main road, where

I must turn one way or the other, must choose
as if my destiny. Right or left, which shall it be.
I have long ago lost north south east west,
the sun leering sometimes behind me, sometimes in front.
Ted sets the table and sits down to read, the soup

on simmer, I roar *left,* he grates the cheese,
Buddy rises on his hind legs, but Ted says No.
No cheese, Buddy, not by the hair of your chinny

chin chin. I am doing well, not yet having run up
against either the Platte or Mount Rushmore.
Ted begins a new chapter, Hattie yawns, Buddy
thinks someone should stir the soup. I see a sign.

It says HALPERN'S ARBORETUM. Ah, a landmark!
I'll call Ted; I'll describe my whereabouts. I whip out
my cellular phone. Hello Ted, I say. Are you lost,
he asks. Near Halpern's Arboretum, I say.

Ted's reply is brilliant, I think, and helpful but
I am not sure, because my cell phone,
always petulant, picks this time to quit. I roll
down the window and take aim, but I do not quite
throw the phone because I begin to notice a prairie
on my left, a beautiful stretch of bluestem,

some stems of which begin to look familiar. Yes.
Black mailbox, yes, Ted's house, yes, but what is it
doing on *that* side of the road? No matter, here's
Ted's right hand extending beyond the rim of the
front porch. Here's his flannel shirt, his beard,
his hug, his plains eye, laconic, blue,
as if home must be close at hand,
dug in, planted, lasting,
perpetually found.

St. Cecilia, Seward County

I kneel to get a better look at St. Cecilia,
at the red line on the mannequin's neck,
the line where the ax, I'm told, would cut off her head.
A better look at St. Cecilia, face down in her purple robe
in her glass case in the Church of the Assumption.
A better look at her light brown hair, given,

the clipping on the wall says, by a pair of sisters
now old women in the county. On my knees
on the green carpet, I wonder if one sister or the other
might kneel here to see their hair, to see the braid
hanging off the saint's shoulder onto the floor,
the hair their father cut with scissors, their mother
somewhere in the house crying, the sisters not
crying because, the clipping says, Father asked,

and we gave. The clipping calls attention
to the saint's hands, a last testament to the trinity,
in death her fingers curling into fists
except one finger on the right, three on the left,

which, the clipping points out, means the three in one.
I decide to drive in the direction of Albrecht's farm,
to head west and south along the Big Blue
to buy a jar of jam from Mrs. Albrecht,
Mrs. Albrecht's hands having last summer

picked plums and dumped them out of the pail
into a huge pot on the stove, her hands
having stirred the fruit and tipped the kettle
at the angle for pouring, her hands having
tightened the lids on the jars. Sure enough

the geese bark almost out of hearing
in high thermals over the county,
wavering westward, small knots
on long black threads. Sure enough, one of
Mrs. Albrecht's daughters plays in the yard,

Mrs. Albrecht herself comes from the smokehouse
where she is between batches of deer sausage,
comes into the store to sell me some jelly,
her reddened hands bringing the jars and
and setting them with a click on the counter,
her left smoothing the ledger page, her right

picking up the ballpoint to record the sale:
2 @ $2.00, plum and strawberry rhubarb.
Sure enough she looks up with a pleasantry
about the day and the geese, her altogether sturdy
face turned to me for a moment, her eyes making me
remember a flash of sky over the Big Blue.
Sure enough when I drive away, Mrs. Albrecht's trees,
the apple, the pear, will hold up their hands,
all their fingers ready to bud and to bloom.

Taking the Baby to the Prairie

for Rosalyn

The wren bubbles over.
The voice of the bob-white
is clear as a glass of water.
Out of sight in last year's grasses,
the pheasant drums his wings.

The baby squints and blinks,
swings her head around to look
when the pheasant crows,
when the swallow dips down.

Stems of switchgrass make a low sound
in the wind: Welcome home.

I lift this child to grassland,
to kingbird,
to cedar and sumac,
to long roots hidden like a deer in the draw.

Under the shells of these dry grasses
a green strength comes.

Nine-Mile Prairie, April

What I like is the sound of my own laugh on the prairie
when two swallows dive-bomb me for walking
too close to their nest.

What I like is the sound of frogs, the just-out-of-mud sounds
of peepers grinding their song as if to sharpen it,
same song, same verse forever.

What I like is the sound of the dove,
mourning an *old-old-old-very-old* loss.

What I like is last year's lespedesa, thin ladies in bonnets
nodding *yes, yes, uhuh, uhuh.*

What I like is last year's indigo: dried up, faded, bent.

What I like is a locust tree, no leaves yet, but sporting—
temporarily—a thrush.

The smell of plum brush so sweet it makes some exquisite nerve ache.

Cottonwoods with wads of nests: hankies close to the bosom.

What I like is when a quail startles me, wants to drag race,
fencerow to zenith in one gasp.

What I don't like is when the dark military airplane rises huge
out of the horizon. What I don't like is the jump of fear on my skin,
but I take a breath and watch it come low over my head. No shark's
mouth opens in its underbelly; it banks left in its ocean, and its
drone drains away.

What I don't like is when a tick is running on my jeans, a red-black
dot on my thigh, and when I brush him off, he doesn't brush, but
flattens and sticks.

What I like is when I find a mound of dirt and I don't know what creature's paws dug it.

What I like is a bob-white on this hill; the larks ringing like bells on the next hill over.

What I like is when a deer shows herself on the ridge,
and I see her and three others running exactly on the horizon,
running on stage, the sky the backdrop, a silent movie,
each deer a small perfect silhouette bounding,
each one bumping in turn over a tiny fence.

What I like is a wind coming up out of the west

What I like is when that wind cools my armpits and cheeks and nape
and blows over my ears, stereophonic,
music like the beginning and the whole entire point of it all:
motif, restatement, coda and conclusion

and when that winds brings to my face
the smell of Nine-Mile Prairie, April,

unbreached, intact
sooty, long-covered.

Prairie, April

like me:
old, new, thawed, moist, ready.

Not So Much Bottom Line as Bluestem

I saw a man hugging his son; he took him in,
rubbed his back, folded him to his own body
in the manner I have seen one person
hold another in dreams,
and I was ashamed how I had a moment before
been promoting myself, trying to get ahead,
selling myself when what matters is close against the ribs
and next to the beating noise of the heart

and I longed to be there, my father rising up
and crossing a distance quickly to hold me,
a warm and loyal space
not so much profit as mystery
not so much increase as Elkhorn
not so much envy as bud
not so much advance as seed.

Today my friend told me he is wearing
his dead friend's reading glasses,
taking up her glasses out of his pocket and
putting them on his face, wearing something she had
held and lifted toward her eyes many times a day
without thinking, glasses she laid on the pages
of her books, glasses she chose and cursed and
looked for when they were lost, folded
like a tidy bundle of twigs on the table,
glasses her eyes looked devilishly over
when she cracked a joke. He said when

he took her to the hospital
that last time, she wanted him to gather up this and that,
and after she had died, there were her reading glasses
in his shirt pocket
as if she herself had tapped them in,
saying, *Here, Babe, it ain't Scotch*

but these will definitely last longer.
My friend is wearing his dead friend's reading glasses and
I want to do that, too, to take up what someone has accidentally

or purposely left me. My friends are
helping me get a little closer,
not so much to conquer as to leaf out
not so much to own as coyote, badger, deer
not so much critic as Niobrara, Missouri, Platte
not so much one-up as switchgrass, sumac,
bluegill, catfish, wolf.

Back and forth they rocked in the room,
the man holding the grown child,
the grown child holding his father,
rocking one another in time
Oh Papa I'm sorry

each come home to this neck and
shoulders, spine and arms
and hand in the hair, rocking
slow as midnight rain.

I saw once on a wide plain a cloud of geese
rising, a spiral in the light,
the geese like hundreds of papers
in a whirlwind, rising, rising,

and I wanted to whirl in that column. I held out my
arms, raised my face
not so much the power as the trail
not so much to garner as to free

and I rock with my father *Papa, oh Papa*

I hold out my arms to the column of birds

I rock back and forth
my mother father friends daughters sons arms hold me,
not so much the market as the daybreak
not the rush but the lake
not so much résumé
but to live
not so much promote as bison, elk,
aquifer, sandhills, snowbank, plum brush.

My friend is wearing his dead friend's reading glasses;
I, too, want to take up something of hers, of yours
something that rested on your skin or hair
something your hand touched.
I want to extend my hand, want you to reach with yours,

as if I can stand close enough to matter
in that radius where we are separate together
not so much impress as honest
not so much merge as search
not so much first as true
not so much to grasp as to fly.

The African American Quilt Exhibit

My lunch date falls through, so I duck into the art gallery
for the African American quilt exhibit. I am alone in a very large room
with quilts on the walls. Beside each quilt a photo of the woman,
or in some cases, women, who put these riots together.

One woman stands in a yard, holds her quilt up for the camera.
She is smiling as if she loved her life.
One quilt has a white line sewn corkscrew fashion
partway across a solid red field. *Corkscrew* not the right word

because *corkscrew* implies symmetry.
Symmetry is too tame, too same.
One quilt is filled with four huge gray mules, square shoulders and hips,
a white eye in each face, but off kilter: in the eyebrow,
in the mane. One quilt is completely covered with sprawling

words and half-words: *the lor is my shaperd*, and again
the lar is my shapper, the multi-colored letters sewn on, the words spelled
differently in each block and more creatively and half gone. *the lard is*
my sh An old woman leaning on her cane comes slowly into the room.

We are strangers but she tells me about her quilts, the first one she made
when she was young. The double wedding ring pattern, she says.
Cottons, whatever I had, she says. Says she *used* her quilts,
couldn't hang them up. I tell her about my quilt, and I tell her
I don't want her to lose her comb; I see it's dangling. So she

brings her hand up and repositions the teeth of the brown comb
into her white silk hair. She doesn't approve, I can tell,
of the less than square edges of the quilts, of the misspelled words,
of the big stitches. I don't contradict her but I move on,

can't get enough of crooked, riot, wild. I like her,
I like talking to her, leaning as she is
on her cane, still huffing from the exertion of the stairs,
but I want to see more, more, all there is, every cockeyed thing,
no dainty little invisible stitches. Let the seams show let them show.

I leave the gallery, stand for a moment on the steps in the winter sun.
It's the first warm day, the red cardinal calls in the white tree,
there is the non-metered drip of water from the building,
the shadows of poles on the worn bricks of the street.
The snow is melting; water spreads on the sidewalk in a hundred

non-symmetrical shapes *the lar is my shepper the lor is my sh*
I stand, eyes closed, with light on my face.
Behind my eyelids a lively orange
where yellow shapes slowly re-configure.
I drink up color like elixir.

The Living, the Warm

Aunt Wilma touches the corpse, touches her Aunt Clara,
lays her old hands on the hands in the casket and says,
Doesn't she look pretty? So pretty, isn't she?
and it is true, Great-Aunt Clara, 99, looks sharp
and Sunday-best in her turquoise blue suit,
ruffles at her wrist and throat, her eyes closed,
her hair anything but stingy, that shade of blue-white

which she and her sisters want, a capsule of bluing
in the rinse water to keep a shade of yellow from stealing in.
Yes, she is pretty, and Aunt Wilma lays her hands on
and keeps them there and looks into her aunt's face
as if they had the afternoon to talk about plums
or pies or the need for rain. As if it were the thing to do,
to lay your hand on the hands of the dead
as my father did

when my grandmother lay in the funeral home.
He invited me, saying *See, she doesn't mind,*
but I shook my head and wiped my eyes
with a Kleenex, not wanting to know
if the body is hard, not wanting to know how cold,
how more or less empty. Maybe my father, the boy,
touched his father's hand, that same gesture,
when the body lay in the house for the night,
perhaps in the living room
on the farm north of the point where the Niobrara
and the Keya Paha flowed, still flow, together.

When my father's body lay in the church,
I came early with my mother; the time was there,
I could have laid my hand on the wrist, maybe his cuff,
or his fingers, one cold nail, or his shoulder.
I could have straightened his already straight tie,
but I didn't. My mother laid her hand on his;

my hand was on her back, the ridges of her spine,
the curve of her shoulders,
the living, the warm.

After the funeral my aunts sit on metal chairs
in the church basement, taking turns talking to
Aunt Hattie, the eldest, blind, holding court,
leading them all in laughter, telling about the time
somebody started off to the Black Hills in the Ford.
They laugh about somebody in a bear suit trying to
keep the kids away from the still. My turn next, so

Hattie's hands take mine, clasp them; I'm what's left,
what's here today of my golden-haired father,
Hattie's laugh that same little waterfall he heard,
her hands small quick birds fluttering and resting.
I wonder how it feels to touch the dead but

I don't want to find out. Chicken, as my aunts
would say, though I've been amazed at myself
lately, driving in a hailstorm like it was nothing,
the leaves beaten off the trees, sticking to the windows,
hail smashing on the windshield and pounding on the roof,
smeared images all around me through the glass.
Trees and grass and the road and the trucks.
Trapped in my car on the road in a hailstorm,
thunder very close, lightning a quick yellow
knife. But I breathe in the smell of the storm
and go right ahead. Not quite scared to pieces,
as my aunts would say. A chain of hands,
coming on down, funeral by funeral. Soon
I'll be laughing at some weak joke, raucous
in a carful of women. I'll move to the back and

let my daughter drive, take my sister's hand or my
niece's. We'll hold hands in the church basement
or town hall. On the table our lunch waiting.

The cup of coffee, the sandwich, the cake—
a plate of cake as necessary downstairs as the sermon
was upstairs. That will be after. But first,
at the casket, when my turn comes, maybe I'll
lift my small useful dry old hands and lay them,
unpolished fingers, cool dry palms,
onto the hands of the others.

The Gold Ring of its Eye

What My Life Is

My life is not the sound of my husband's breath in sleep,
buttoning and unbuttoning itself,
not the screen door flapping shut, my son
coming home safe from Omaha.
Have the two of you had your first fight yet,
an important thing, the shape your fighting takes,
I would say to my son, if it were
any of my business.
But I'm trying to live my life, not
my son's life, his problems
not to be taken from him,
as I would not take the old harness,

the one he is restoring, repairing
the rivets where they have given way.
That is his, the junctures and joinings.
The grove of hackberries more nearly my life,
young hackberries with knobby bark,
slim leaves clustered together,
small hard berries worthless for eating,

my father building his house
without chopping the hackberries down,
carrying a pail of water to each one
in a stretch of dry weather,
maybe after a ten-hour day,
housebuilding being nearly his life,
and I love to watch on TV
those shows where a man and a woman
in protective glasses and gloves
use a staple gun or a tape measure,
take off old wallboard with a crowbar,
but that is not my life, someone else's

houses, what they can build or fly,
not the ideas my son can understand
from the heavy law books in his lap.
He sits in a chair, studying,
in one room or another,
those books weighting him down,
keeping him from floating up and off.
Not what he studies from the books
or the computer screen, none of that

my life either, though sometimes I check out
all the books on one subject or one poet,
bring them home on the bus,
pile them on the floor, lie on the couch
and eat them systematically,
the turning of pages a sound
against my stomach, my hand
smoothing a page. That is not my life.
The people I call on the weekends,
my daughter and my mother, agreeing with them,
asking the next question, sometimes

making each of them laugh,
wanting to stay in touch and not
be a nuisance, that is not my life.
The notebooks where I have highlighted
in yellow, or where I have kept on writing
in the dark and can hardly read it,
that is not my life, nor critiquing others,
although it is a pleasure I won't deny
myself. My life is almost
the summers of childhood.
Long summers of bicycles
and one cousin's Boston terrier and
another cousin's cap gun, the mud
we put into jar lids and decorated

with mint leaves and white flowers
that grew on my grandmother's cellar,
the bushel baskets of jars she had brought

from the farm but no longer canned
full in summer. She still baked her bread.
It is almost her bread, her hands unwrapping
the loaf from the tea towel, cutting slices for me
one after another, never saying
you've had too many or that's enough,
one after another, sliced thin and
fragrant, sometimes a big air hole
near the brown crust, big enough
to put my finger through.
When she cut the next slice
it fell over onto the board silent as a leaf.
The days fall easy, the days
sweet, like this evening when my
husband and I went to a certain park,
drove half an hour, and a detour,
to get to the park where we used to walk
twenty years ago. Those nights
we would drive our separate cars
and meet in the moonless night,
that moment when a man
crunched in the darkness up the path toward me,
the white of his t-shirt a dim light,
no way to be sure it was him
until his voice
and the size of his back under my hands,
that hull of solid warm length and curve.
Perhaps that is it, whatever my hands

have pressed and made a soft voice
rubbing over. Is that it,
coming back after twenty years
to do something again

for the fun of it
and then writing of it later
in a notebook in the night
when I should be sleeping,
no music in the house except
the pen over the flat back of the paper,
making up my life in the dark.

The White Lamb in the Yard

Morning after morning you left the farmhouse,
carried your young son to the babysitter.
The child cried, cried like a lamb.
You yourself were a lamb,
meadow to corral to dirty barn.
You want to blame yourself but
a lamb is a lamb is a lamb. Do your work,
cavort, run with ignorance on the spring grass.
White coat, beautiful unscratched eyes,
clean pink mouth, teeth like buds,

like kernels of white corn.
It was your son who cried, and you.
What else could you do?
You scrubbed the pockmarked linoleum,
you waxed it on the weekends, the wax pooling
in the round dents from the chair legs. You carried the clothes
to the wash line, you made the macaroni and tomatoes, you read him
a story, you must have, you must have read him a story.
You did not take a walk in the country.
You were a lamb, not a Jane Austen,
you carried your child on your hip,

you loved him, you didn't know anything, so much of it like that night
your husband said *Where do you keep the blankets?*
You hardly woke up, you were bone weary, woke only if the baby cried.
There's been an accident on the highway. They need blankets.

You told him where the blanket was
and went back down into sleep
because this, like the others,
must be only a bad dream.

The Muse is a Little Girl

The muse is a little girl, impossibly polite.
She arrives when you're talking
or walking away from your car.
She's barefoot, she stands
next to you, mute; she taps your sleeve,
not even on your skin, just touches the cloth
of your plaid shirt, touches it twice.
She feels with her index finger the texture
and you keep talking, or you don't.
She will wait one minute. She is not hungry
or unhappy or poor. She goes somewhere else
unless you turn and look at her
and write it down. I'm kidding.
She's a horse you want to ride, she's a tall horse,
she's heavy, as if she could bear armor.
You can't catch her with apples.
I don't know how you get on.
I remember my cold fingers in the black mane.

Often He Came to Pick Up His Wife

Often he came to pick up his wife,
waited easily, not trying to impress anybody.
And now he is dead,
the vest flat, the tie over it,
the hands unflinching. His face
thin, glasses big, his lips
like carved painted wood.

Near the end at home
in that bag of pain,
he could not lie comfortably.
His daughter placed the pillows:
two under his knees,
two for his arms to drape over,
two to prop up his back and head
for breathing. He was,
as always, grateful.

I want it, this sitting up in bed to write,
this stuffing myself with apples, with bread.
I want it to matter.

Teaching Me to Write

I had a great view of the world
four desks back from the teacher,
a great view of the globe,
and especially of the hole in the Pacific Ocean
below the Tropic of Capricorn.
The teacher said *Write a story*
and so I did. I put Luther in it

because Luther was tall enough to reach
the base of the globe. He was thin
and pale in the next row,
faint patterns like frost on a window
on the back of his close-cut blond head,
white eyebrows when he turned around.
He was a mystery and I put him into my story.
The story didn't say much about
Luther; it left him quiet,
hardly putting two words together
in class or out on the swings or baseball diamond,
but it made Luther personally responsible
for a hole in the Pacific Ocean, made him
guilty but not unloved.

The teacher liked it, hole and all.
Luther said nothing
so I went on to a new page about
a girl who looked like me,
pony-tail and glasses,
who wanted red shoes
more than anything in the world.
Near the bottom of the page I finished the story
in a flash on the last blue line,
the pencil moving fast against the flat white paper,
the shoes almost real enough to weigh down a flimsy box,

their red leather smooth and unscratched in the tissue paper.
When she read it from her place in that tilting hemisphere
Mrs. Fischer laid down her pen and looked at me
as though she might see me, across a distance,
shod in true vermillion.

What She Taught Me

She taught me linking verbs, predicate nouns,
long division, have a Kleenex ready, an apple
a day. She taught me three-quarter time, Greenwich

Mean Time. She taught me *do re mi*, Mexicali Rose,
Rose, Rose, my Rose of San Antone. She taught me
Peas Peas Peas Peas, Eating Goober Peas.
She taught me that a peanut is a goober pea

in certain parts of the world, that it is fine
for things to be different in different parts
of the world, no two goobers alike in their

dry red skins, their pock-marked pods,
that there are latitudes and longitudes we have
never seen, that she had seen some part,
and so would I, that I need not

forego either the swings or baseball, that spelling
is on Friday and it is OK to learn more
than one list, including the hard list; it is not

showing off—it is using what you have.
That using what you have will not please
everybody, that marrying a man of a different stripe

is not a popular thing in a small town in the fifties,
and divorcing and coming home with a child
is even worse, and that you
get up every morning anyway,
and do your work.

Dear Writing,

Where have you been? Where are you when I
need you? People see me here in the Mill
at a table with two notebooks and a motley
cheap pen. They may think I am a friend of
yours. They may think O Writer! Wow!
But I am writing a grocery list or I am
staring at a poster and making
a succession of little dents around
the bottom of my styrofoam cup.
"I don't want to interrupt you from your
writing," the lady says, stopping by my
table, "but I wanted to say how much I
enjoyed your book. I see you are writing
so I won't bother you."
                                        So bother me.
I am only pretending to be writing.
Nobody can *be* writing. We are just
ourselves, our own phony selves
trying to look like writers, sponging air-
conditioning off our favorite coffeehouse,
listening to their CD's, our chairs squeaking,
our bifocals lying on their tables. We look up
from pushing the pens back and forth;
we catch a stranger's eye. I'm writing,
we say with one eyebrow, or with
the turn of the empty empty page.
I drink another cup of decaf
and count the change in my pocket.
I can afford two more days of writing.
The time spent not writing is very important

to the writing, the writing book says.
Good, I say, I'll have a chocolate biscotti.
If I can stick it out until 3:00, I'll have a
blueberry muffin and a peach spritzer.

With any luck at all, a nonwriter will
come over and talk to me and apologize
for taking me away from my writing.
Dale is roasting coffee—he *looks*
like he's reading the paper and checking
his watch, but he's roasting coffee, and
I'm writing. I'm writing the great American
cafe poem. I have ten minutes left to go.

The Light that Makes the Web Show Up

I'll just start writing; I'll just keep
writing until an idea comes like a big white
short-hair dog and sits down, waiting
for me to notice him, pat his head. He sits
down, as I said, and he blinks his eyes. I notice
he doesn't have eyelashes and he does have
a collar. He is probably an editor for a prestigious
publishing house. Now that is a stupid idea. I'll

keep writing while one stupid idea after another
comes along and sits on its haunches. Dingbat.
Slingshot. Dadgum. I'm trying to remember
an interesting word I heard on public radio,
a word a Mormon said about getting on the trail.
I can't remember the word he said. I'll just
keep writing until I remember the dadgum word,
until it comes and sits on its haunches and
washes its black and white face with its lily-
white paw, licking the paw and pushing it
around on its face into the little dents under
its eyes. It will run away if I say a loud word.
If I say *scat* it will start and put its paw down and

roll off the table like a glass jar falling. I'll just
keep writing until I think of something. Have I
thought of something? I've thought of a man
lying on his couch with a notebook at four in the
morning. I'll think of his lead pencil making
small letters into a medium-sized word, a
hyphen, another medium-sized word. I see his
hand and the pencil and the wavy line he draws
under *deer* and *headlight*. In the meantime I
keep waving this pen point above the paper, I

keep digging a little wobbly trough left to right.
I think of writing with my left hand. I hate to
but I will. Even my left hand doesn't have a
speech to make. It bobs along a great deal like
a pigeon. Or a mourning dove. Do you
know how much trouble it is to say *mourning dove*
left-handed? The dot at the end of the sentence
is a poke. Poke. Poke. What would happen if I
wrote *California*? Behold, it waves like a row

of palm trees. I'll just keep writing until my left
arm falls off. You don't even have to have an
idea in your head. You don't have to have an
end in mind. I'll just keep writing, mind or no
mind. I'll write as if I had a predetermined
orbit. I'll write as if I had a cause. I'll write
past the time I should quit. I'll keep going. I'll

write about my grandmother what not again well
its better than writing about your father again.
I'll write about my father. I'll write about him
if I want to. I'll write about my knee or the
prime minister or the prime minister's knee. I'll
write about trees cedar pine palm elm oak
Christmas telephone double. I'll write about
cats though I know nothing. I'll remember a cat or
make one up. I'll put him on the backstairs or

the roof—that'll surprise him. I'll put him
smackdab that's not the word the Mormon said
but it's close smackdab into a movie with Jimmy
Stewart. Jimmy Stewart looks like a cat:
surprised, wide-eyed that life would cross him.
I'll put the cat in a toothpaste ad wearing
glasses, the cat not the ad. I'll put the cat
into a jewelry case in Klein's Jewelers in Broken Bow,
Nebraska. I'll put the cat into a culvert in Bethany

Park. Even if I do that, I'll have absolutely
nothing to write about. It's one of those star-
crossed days nothing has occurred to me.
Maybe I need a couch and a clock chiming four.
But look, I'm writing. Poking dots at the end of
each thought; each stupid thought gets its own
dot. I bet some people in this room if
questioned would say I look like I am writing.
They are fooled. I am wearing down my pen. I am

practicing my push-pulls. I am thinking of cats,
left-handed. I am thinking of a man who reads a
paperback, bent over it as if catching a frog.
I am thinking about the prairie, a thrush
in the tallest cottonwood. A thrush, not a bluebird.
A bluebird concentrates, keeps still if it has
nothing to say. Not me, nor this thrush. We
keep saying the same thing, a syllable or two,

over and over and we repeat it just to hear the
sound of it. Big-bodied thrush, not a lark.
The lark, beautiful, musical, writes as if she's
swallowed small bells at the end of her sentences.
That was a stupid sentence. I'll just keep
writing breakneck speed like a herd of horses
black and white and piebald stocky ugly little
mustangs galloping, raising dust.

What the Moon Wants

I won't climb out of bed
as if it were my horizon. I won't
stagger in dew-wet grass,

face up, my eye and her eye.
I'm not the moon's favorite
hunting dog. I will not

pad out to the yard to
see what she wants,
my pale feet
wading the cold white current.

We'll Drive the Olds

We'll drive the Olds.
She can take the pastures
without benefit of highway.
When we get to the pond we'll
park and listen to the frogs
squandering their unlearned song.
Three deer will run and stop

and run again in the tallgrass.
I'll call them omens. I'll
call them signs. The dark will
arrive, warm armfuls of stars,
nape and skin and breath of stars,
you meanwhile imagining a complexion

for the moon, that white
bird below the horizon;
I meanwhile convincing myself
that the two of us
in the epicenter of this abundance
have only tonight.

I Don't Want to Speak Car

I don't want to know radiator, coolant,
block, piston, accelerate. Brake shoe,
hood. I don't even want to know *hood.*
I don't mind chauffeur, taxi, airplane,
but I don't want to hear a syllable of car,

not even auto-mo-beel. Not fan belt,
gasoline, gasohol, additive. I don't want
to hear a whisper of it, not antifreeze, seat
cover, factory installed. I don't like wing
vent, running board, headlight. I hate
chrome. Two door. Detroit. Deal.

Ford. Mercury. Cad. I hate tread.
I hate jack. I hate the little nuts that
hold the wheels on. I hate windshield, front
and back. I hate list price, package, and
dash. This town, if I had my joy-ride
Pennzoil way, would sit up to its axles
in Carhenge.

In No Hurry

I'm thinking about my husband holding the garage door
off his car the time when he'd pressed the button and
the door was coming down, going to hit the trunk of the
car, not pulled in far enough. He never considered not
stepping in to take a beating from the door, to hold it up
on his forearms, the door that threatened something he

cared about. He will take a beating for
what he cares about, hold the door, hold off anything,
if he can. He cares about lasting, outlasting.
The door pushing down on his forearms as if on a
shelf. He stands there as long as it takes. As long as it
takes, that's how long he'll stand there and take it,
hold it until the belt cracks or the motor quits,
the door trying to come down and the man

holding it up as long as it takes. No one to help.
I've read advice: eat when you eat and sleep when you
sleep, hold the garage door up when you hold the
garage door up. Just write when you're writing. Not
how do I like this cheap pen, how is my handwriting,
are my eyes going blind, do I have some bit of
broccoli in my teeth, could it have been there
when I talked. Is there an afterlife or are we sparrows
flying through a barn, flying into the hayloft and on out
the other side, when it's over it's over. How can I

enjoy the time I have left and do I then sink back into
the earth like a tulip bulb or maybe like an annual.
My husband holding that door up with his body for as long
as it takes, trying at first to heave the door upward hard
to make the machine reverse, but something wrong with
the mechanism, his arms later swollen in a wide band
where the door ground against them. Noticing thoughts
and letting them go. Let a thought into my mind, one

thought at a time in as if through a window, see it, let it
go out the other window, not analyzing, just sitting
with my thoughts, like now, not trying to write fast,
because my thoughts are not fast, staying with them
as he did with the garage door, his back strong, doing
weights twice a week for years, five minutes on the
garage door not much as weights go, his back and his
legs and his forearms doing what he tells them to do,
wanting to do it, why not, life is the speed it is, as my
breath is the speed it is. I wonder if my friend with

cancer watches her breath. I wonder if she has been
able to forget she has cancer, if there have been a few
minutes in the past month when she has been free of it
in the back of her mind. I wonder if she will die
from it. I wonder if she will live and be changed.
I wonder what her friends should do and say.
As a 3-D picture makes an image: the curved solid backs
of dolphins suddenly appearing, their forms leaping in the space
where colored marks had been. I wonder if my
life is like that, a three-dimensional picture, if I could
let my eyes go slack and see it, if I could look at it
as long as it takes.

While I Sleep

While I sleep my mother
sews a skirt for me,
a vest to match,
her press cloth a strip of grocery bag.
My father sits in the recliner,
cop show rattling

the edges of evening,
neighbor's pickup hunkering by,
gravel crunching,
dust rolling up into the dark.
She dips a rag into water, wrings it,

draws it again across the paper.
I sleep the foolish sheets of love,
steam and the brown smell
rising to her face.
I sleep the foolish sheets of love,

yet to come the narrow bed
of marriage. Rough places
of her fingers catching on the cloth,
iron hissing down the length,
my mother presses, she sews.

Father

his head for the first time lies on a satin pillow
they have trimmed his nails shorter than he ever did
but he would not mind
tolerant even now
of another man's way of doing things

his arm was larger, rounder
lying across the wheel
to guide the whining truck
three-quarters up the hill
the door open, the gravel of the road edge
and wet low bushes crawling by
he looking back at the trees and the trailer
saying calmly jump if we jack-knife
you'll be all right

his arms bulging under short sleeves rolled twice
his head resting against the wiry red hair of the cow
keeping the rhythm of the milk
cutting lines into the foam

or on the scaffold against the new wall
lifting the concrete block, turning it,
fitting it into the pattern
tilting the blade of the trowel
tapping the block with the handle

his face is free of all the things he should have done
he should have bought his father's farm
he should have joined the union
he should have gone fishing in south carolina
with young Eddie

but when the dirt falls on the curved polished lid
when it slides off the shovel
like a hand opening to let something go
everything will be all right
all things are as they should be

I would like to touch again
the rounding of his arm
put my fingers into the L of his elbow

cover his hand
as he showed me in Kramer's mortuary
that grandmother did not mind being touched
and that those dead, and living, are not untouchable
if you are not afraid

Otto

who stood at the edge of family pictures
the moving shade of the oak tree
blotching his face
whose hands held his gray felt hat
behind him, rolling the brim
toward the sweat band
whose brown suit grew
season by season too large
each harvest inching farther down
on his wrists toward the large nubs of his knuckles

whose skin on his high cheekbones
shone in the light from the window
as they figured God's Acre
on the tablecloth
whose voice caught at the start of his sentences
like a plow settling into a new furrow
who did not sing in church
his very clean hands folded over his knees

who on summer afternoons
poured cold coffee into his white cup
who said he liked it

who owned a bed in his brother's farmhouse
(no flop-ear brown dog running to the gate
ever known as Otto's
no pipe
no International
no bad jokes
no twenty-two
no girl as far as anybody said
no child of his
crying or sleeping on the second floor
in the dark house)

who before reaching up for his hat
on the nail above the separator
would stand
mornings
at the screen door
his hands in his back pockets

At the Derby Star

I knew this guy once, went to Europe
supposed to go with three girls
they chickened out so he went by himself
takes a lot of guts
not knowing the language

you take your vacations
some people drive to the Grand Canyon
get out, take their picture in front of their car
they get back
they say: wanna see my pictures?

me, I drive out of the county once in a great while
I throw a beer can out of the car
come back, that's my vacation

heard on the radio the average man
dies at the age of 69
the average woman lives to 72
wonder why that is

course, you take your averages
you stand one leg in a bucket of hot water,
the other in cold,
on an average, you should be comfortable
but you're not

A Man in Love With Wind

for Don Welch

A man in love with wind
held a noun in his hand
to admire the layers of its feathers,

the gold ring of its eye.
He spoke to it, hoping it heard. He tossed it
up onto a shelf of air,

where it opened and
rolled into flight: upstroke, downstroke.
It left him. Now he listens

for the one that will circle, the one
that even in the dark will land,
will place its weightless

claws on the shingles.
In his ear a sound so delicate
it must mean breath, it must mean

home,

home.

Frying Eggs in Bacon Fat

Frying the eggs in bacon fat
the next morning, she thinks about it.
She doesn't like to think about it,
the river filling her mouth and throat,
her hands clawing the dark water,
clawing his arm; he was mad

about that, the scratches on his arm
and he was mad about the ring,
said he'd never buy her another,
said she had one if she could
find it on the bottom of the Niobrara.
In part of her mind

she thinks it was not her fault,
they shouldn't have been
pushing on her head and laughing,
her husband, his brother,
but men did that sort of thing.
It was supposed to be fun,
cooling off in the river.
Nothing can make them sorry,

not the least bit apologetic.
She bastes the eggs,
blindfolding them the way
he likes, splashing bacon grease

over them with her mother's
old spatula. The yolks
whiten in the hot fat,
the brown flecks
catch and hold. Maybe with time
he'll come to be more loving and kind.

The Saucepan, Washed

The saucepan, washed,
rinsed, dried, put into its place,
its place and no other.
No, that did not keep her safe,
not the dishtowels, white, bleached, folded,
ironed. The crockery, the pots,
the recipes refined.

The wind blows the brown oak leaf
across the stubborn snow.

I'm cooking for company today:
Three pies: apple, lemon, chocolate.
The frosting hardens—
but not too hard—
over a batch of brownies.
This is what she did, isn't it?

She loved her patterned plates,
her graceful cups,
her extra sugar bowl.

She died before she was completely ready,
before she saw the children in their fine clothes,
arranged for the camera.

A crow barks again and again;
the yucca shakes in the wind.
Maybe she wiped her hands on a towel
and stood for a minute
in front of whatever window there was.

Losing

I lost the opal earrings, gift of love, left
in the pocket of a bathrobe, washed away
in a soapy stream down the slick dark pipes.
When I lost the turquoise earrings,
I said *They will return, they will return*
the mantra having worked before
but not this time.

I lost a bracelet, new heavy
silver band, small turquoise egg
over my young wrist. I left it in a Phillips 66
restroom, a lucky find for the next girl
or perhaps she gave it to the clerk at the counter
in case we came back which we didn't.
Miles down the road I thought of it, stricken,
my father chalking it up to experience,
to learning the hard way. I didn't learn,
left my sunglasses hanging on a soap dispenser,

my black cateye sunglasses, the black veneer
having rubbed off where my fingers
held them to put them on, the white showing
through the paint where my fingers
from habit touched them. We touch
each other's faces
here
and here,
earlobe
lips

thumb and index finger
here and here

softly along the line of the jaw
eroding surely the shape of what we will lose.

Hawk Over Snow

Washing My Hair in the Platte

As if submerging a flower,
he dips my head into the river. I sit up streaming,
the water of the Platte in my ears, my eyes,
its sand moving under my body. He begins

to wash me, taking his time,
the shape of his hands taking
a measure of my temples,
of my skull, of my neck.
The small bones under the skin.
His fingers in the hair
at the nape. Smoothing lather
away from forehead,
smoothing chin, throat.
His palm on the top of my head
as if in blessing.

A puff of soap loose on my cheek,
his fingers corralling it.
The sticks of his fingers
slowly over my cheeks,
over my shoulders.
His eyes at the precise

level for studying him
in the river. The sun
on his skin a definition.
The sheen of his eye,
the wiry hairs of his mustache.
His eyebrows. The cup of his ear.

Videotaping the Total Lunar Eclipse

We watched the eclipse from our driveway.
My husband was in his stockingfeet, hadn't
planned to stay, didn't bring his coat,
stood close to me, stood behind me
and around me like a second shawl,
his chest warm, his back cold.
He was hooked, couldn't make himself
go in, the moon holding him, shoeless.
He went in for the video camera and still
didn't put on his shoes. For Mom, he said.
He filmed and talked, a running lunar
commentary. I don't know
if this will turn out
at all, filming like this. I don't know
if there is enough light for you to see.

He makes films, show them to her
Wednesday nights since she's been ill. He films
his grandson. It's still Saturday, he says. It's
about 4:00. Calvin is having a snack. Eat
hearty, Calvino.

It's not a story until he tells it,
like the travelogues she used to watch at the Cooper
or the Stuart, somebody at the podium in the dark
talking about Venice while the film runs.
He makes a story, tells her what she's

seeing as she sees it. This is Calvino
in his new shirt eating Cheerios. This is
Calvino in his swing. Hang on, Boy.

She hasn't been there until her guide,
that flickering point of view, tells the story.

This is Venice. These houses were built
in the 1700's. It was a beautiful sunny day.
The moon is three-quarters covered now. I don't
know if you can see it. I don't know if
there's enough light but we'll give it a try.

This Ain't No Bass Boat Day

My love is in the shower,
his elbows banging the sides,
the shower small as the cabin is small,
the woods huge around the cabin, around me,

waiting in bed as I am
for my love to be done in the shower,
my love already done with fishing—
three big walleye keepers, two
thrown back—my love having already
walked down to the boat in the dark, having
already fished and come back, he says,
victorious. Ready now for a romp,
he says, in this haystack I've been keeping warm.

Haystack, nothing, I say. More like, I declare,
a whole darn marina. This ain't no 16-foot Lund day.
Consult your almanac. If luck holds, if the wind is right,
this could be your twenty-footer inboard/outboard day;
this could be your off-shore racer day.
With any luck at all, I tell him, this could be your
open seas day, your unlimited hydroplane V-8
with supercharger day. This ain't no snark day,

no jonboat on top of the car day. This ain't no
Yellow Jacket 9.9 Evinrude day. You can start hoping,
I tell him, for a twin-hulled Hobie Catamaran day.
The moon perched as it was for luck last night,
a golden grossbeak above the flat dark lake,
you might hope for your 40-foot
three-deck Grady White day. And later,
if luck holds, if the wind is right,

we'll have a late breakfast in town at the cafe.
If luck holds, if the wind is right, maybe our ultimate
good luck charm, the town eccentric, will return.
He'll come into the cafe, bow to the waitress,
his green cap pulled down on his forehead
like a good omen, and he'll shuffle in his skinny-leg way
to his favorite booth in the back,
sprinkling our future good fortune right and left,
singing and shuffling, shuffling and singing—
only slightly off-key—
I don't know why I love you like I do.
I don't know why; I just do.

The Caffeine Kicks In

> *Old friend old friend of mine,*
> *I won't quit you. Those blues I've known them too.*
> *—John Walker*

Saturday we're on the road early
and the caffeine kicks in, so he
begins to talk about work. It's Boiler Repair 101
for me in the car rolling east at dawn,

the long drive ahead of us like the sunrise,
which is trying to outdo itself:
a Mormon Tabernacle Choir flying buttress
and gold filigree display; rays through the clouds

like a giant fan on the horizon over Iowa.
Here in the car, he's explaining
clevis, chainfall, redhead, and *come-along.*
Life spreads over me and

around me, a shower of golden light.
There's nothing like a workingman
and his coffee and a road trip.
Quick, lay that bluegrass CD

into the doohickey. I need everything
at once. I need Stone Pony Blues
I need the Sand Hills Rag I need

Old friend old friend of mine
I won't quit you. Those blues I've known them too.

I need music, I need summer,
I need morning, 70 degrees, humid.
This day, like a particular geode,
about to break open and warm up.

The Cleaning Wind

A cleaning wind blew into my office.
You call this an office? it said.
Who asked you, I said.
It was a cold wind, it chilled
the chairs and the floor,
sifted my papers,
lifted them out of the stacks,
floated them out the window,
a flock of white birds migrating.

A gum wrapper I was saving,
a post card with loons on it, a stamp with Alfred Hitchcock,
the journals of Anais Nin I never got around to reading,
two boxes of double-sided double-density disks,
the overpriced platypus my daughter bought me,
the box of small envelopes,
the box of medium-sized envelopes,
the box of business-sized envelopes.

Don't touch my photographs, I said.
The wind quivered them. I thought they'd
had it: Don with his coffee cup,
Don with his hands in his pockets at Lake Andes,
Don on a boulder on Long's Peak. Take my telephone, I said,

clean it out, move the walls,
get rid of these files, bring in a bird cage,
a molting green parrot repeating over and over
Good work, Excellent work.
I want something out of this, I said.
I want a pony—make it a brown and white Shetland—

I want a bowl of apples, very red,
very cold, the juice locked in, waiting.
I want a collie, I want my sister to come for a visit.
Take this e-mail, I said. Take this book review.
Bring in a chamber orchestra, an eclipse,
a hippo. Come on, you chicken wind,
show me what you've got.

Prairie Pretends to be Mild

Prairie trots out her February hoax, her melt down,
her best dress for the blind date. But I'm not blind.

Still, here are her cafes, the doors open to the street.
I'm not throwing my mittens away. She's so

coy, her rivers wearing only a little ice,
the provocative slip showing. Trust me,

Prairie says, I love you. And she does,
her switchgrass lying down with whispers

in a western breeze. Trust me too, I answer.
Wrap me in grasses, call to me with cranes

and plovers, snowgeese, meadowlarks.
Watch me with the quiet lover's eyes

of kingbirds. Hold me, child and woman,
rock me, your wild indigo tangled in my hair.

Holed Up In Valentine, Nebraska

The window of my room on the second floor of the Comfort Inn
shows trees near the alley flailing their skinny arms.
Wind out of the north 30 to 40, gusting to 50,
the face in the TV says. I can say it blew the sunrise
all the way to gray. The third snowplow since 5:45

grinds by on the highway. Here I am,
holed up in Cherry County: poet-in-the-schools,
schools closed on account of snow,
plenty of paper and pretzels, plenty of time,
plenty of hours to write a chapbook on anything handy.
Or iron all my socks.

The wind swirls the skirt of snow on the roof of the lumberyard.
A couple of black dogs don't give a darn for blizzard conditions,
for total accumulations. They chase each other out of sight.
The ice machine in the hall dumps its paydirt
into its lap as it did all day yesterday.
There's something new here, must be.

There's a waffle machine at the self-serve breakfast downstairs,
and poppy seed muffins. They're pretty good, the nice lady
from Fargo tells me. She's snowed in too,
on her way to Phoenix. I imagine the Niobrara,

lying low in her white banks while this thing blows over.
I imagine a Charolais or an Angus, head-down,
turning tail to the wind. Out of the snowbank
at the edge of the parking lot, a single stalk of dry prairie grass
flops like a metronome. Thirty to forty, with gusts to 50.
Life blows on.

Yes, These Are My People

I point to my bagel in the box of bagels, warm,
steaming up the plastic, point to one with a raisin bump.
The clerk is young, big-boned, round-cheeked,
big overalls, dark hair, plenty of it, plenty of

everything. I'd say she'd be the face in a European
painting of a certain era, if I knew such things.
If I knew such things, I'd place her in a certain
painting by a certain European master, but I place her
here, at least for now, my town, my sidewalks,
my cold skies, my kid in two layers of coats,

both unzipped, on his way to school. My pickups
coasting up to the stop sign, my bell hanging on the door
of the coffeeshop, ringing me in, ringing me out.
My people, my town, my bread. The spaces in the
bagel, the circle of it—two circles of it—toasted.
The dark soft raisin, the tough crust.

I chew. I'm home.
My men at the construction site across the street,
their yellow hardhats, their gray sweatshirts,
the arms of one signalling to the truckdriver backing in.
The truckdriver trusting only what he can see:
the semaphore arms, the come-hither gesture
of the gloved hand.

Thinking of Emily Dickinson

Go away, mosquito. I'll put you
in some other poem.
For this one, I'm writing the jays and flickers,
the heavy smell of ragweed,
and the hunch of the shoulders of the kingbird.
Plums, yellow, bulbous,
under the fingers of the slender leaves.

There must have been hordes of women
whose work we'll never know,
and yet they did it.
An army of Emily Dickinsons, scattered.
They filled their pages with the dark ink,
their poems simple, common, full of mistakes,
full of feeling,
full of love for the bees and stamens of the world.

There Are Poems in Every Tree

There are poems in every tree, every
piece of ribbon waving on any mailbox.
Does this not overcome you,
the sheer abundance of it?

The low sound of dry leaves hanging on
in the wind in every pin oak along
the sidewalk that lies before you.
Every man in a tee-shirt coming out his door
to get his garbage can. He trundles it
back toward his house and you walk on.
Daffodils, beloved yellow fools, are showing
above ground again. There are small new leaves,

folded and creased, in the neighbor's hedge.
Now a crow draws a straight line
from one tree to another, flaps to a landing
in a big locust, and tells the world—
detail, detail, detail—all about it.

Lying on the Driveway, Studying Stars

Through the eye of binoculars
stars are not steady;
they quiver minutely
as muscles in tired arms

and Cassiopeia is taken apart,
each separate star
swimming to you in a small round sky,
bobbing, giddy, before becoming quiet:

a young woman in a distant city
crying.

To Leave My Grandma

To leave my grandma, I didn't want it. The woman,
Kosovar, displaced, interviewed by American radio:
To leave my grandma, I didn't want it. That's the truth.
And her voice sinks into the radio and the rest of the day.
Me, I'm picking up pieces of glass at my mailbox, the soft rain

sinking into my coat. Me, I'm walking on the wet sidewalk.
I'm cutting through a park to a cafe where I'm such a regular
that one waitress asks me to sign the farewell card for another
who's moving to Kansas City just for the heck of it. A cafe
where I've been having decaf and toast through several sets
of hostesses, waiters, and cooks. And what I can't

forget is what she said about the train ride. Or what she couldn't
finish saying about the soldiers. The boy who was crying on the train.
Couldn't stop crying for his father. They had killed his father.
He couldn't stop crying. The soldiers opened the window.
They pushed the boy through the window. I open the unreal
square of strawberry jelly. I eat.

No Greenhouse Flowers For Your Grave

At your head I place an armful of something old-fashioned:
lilacs, peonies, white blossoms of the snowball bush,
the real thing, white globes of the kind that make my nose itch.

You were the real thing, you are the real thing,
here in your plot six feet under.
Bones and hair, whatever is left, stuck to satin.
A real thrush echoes and echoes himself in the cedar tree.
It's spring, time to move on. Cucumbers sprout
in the garden. Peas soon, and the radish.
Soon you will rise up, young father of three,

you will take your lunchbox and go
to your pickup parked under the cottonwoods.
You have a job to do.
You have your work, work is the sinews of the body,
work holds you up like bones.

You will drive to work, your face in the window:
blue eye, pointed chin, shock of hair. I bring you
back because I can. I give you crows, cardinals,
wren, thrush, robin, jay.
Listen: dead is winter. You are going strong.

Summer, Striking

At just the right time my father struck the mortar,
struck being the proper term for the gentle motion
of smoothing the seams between the blocks,
the mortar set up but not yet hard,
this necessary striking that was not striking at all
and sometimes he let me do the striking, child hanging around, helping.

He was laying blocks for a building in the country,
he and I the only humans,
nothing nearby but pasture, a road,
a stand of trees, a plowed field, a herd of Angus.

Not much good as helper, I could not
lift the blocks into their places on the wall.
I could fetch the blue chalk line, I could
lug a half-pail of *mud*, his term for mortar.
I was not a true assistant those long days in the sun,
the new wall taking shape course by course,

the birds one by one into the trees,
cardinals mostly, and jays,
their morning songs when we began,
their twilight sounds when we called it quits

but it's the noontime I remember, that long and drowsy hour
when we ate the sandwiches and rested.

Stretched out in the grass under the cottonwoods,
his cap over his face, he dozed; I played with pebbles,
made a row of stones, listened to the silence,
watched a jet make a thin white contrail.

This was the time between,
this was the mortar, the joints,
and we struck it lightly, gave it shape:

two small figures,
one in the shade, reclining,
one in the sun, standing, looking up, shielding her eyes,
alone on a shimmering plain.

You Gave Me A Typewriter

You gave me a typewriter for Christmas. Before I
unwrapped the box, I thought it was an accordian. I think

you had asked me which I wanted. I think I didn't know.
I think I said *Either.* I was young, high-school,

so much space, as now, between *know* and *don't know.*
I didn't know what was in the package, a present for me,

oldest daughter, nerdy, egg-head, interested in music,
no piano in the house, my uncle's accordian heavy when

it hung on my young neck, when I tried to move my wrists
and hands as he had moved his over the array of buttons,

over the white keys and the black. How his fingers found
those buttons in their rows, pushed one at a time,

quick and off, how his eyes could stay on the sheet music
while he played, while he pulled the instrument open

and pushed it back. *Lady of Spain*
stretched out, lengthened, shook,

and folded up again, the music filling the spaces
between the walls, under and over the table

and chairs, the top of the freezer and the stove.
Perhaps a small accordian for me in the package, my

Christmas present, my gift, special, and I tried
to be glad it was the gray case of a gray typewriter,

a Remington, portable, something I needed.
Did you want an accordian, you asked me.

No, I said. I'll play this.

As Long As Someone Remembers

I remember the round shape of the ward,
the nurse's station in the center, the young nurse
Rhonda, a South Dakota girl, soft-hearted,
I remember the blue sweater she wore over
her uniform. The ward was cold. She said
she'd scrounge around for more blankets.
She brought five of them, white cotton
hospital blankets for us, to keep him warm
and also at night for my mother in
the brown chair by the bed. He wasn't eating.
Maybe he had decided Enough is enough,
but then his old buddy Curly came and talked to him,
Curly in the brown chair, talking to
the silent man in the bed.

Rhonda's eyes filled with tears the morning
she knew he wasn't going to make it, but first
there was the morning he decided to eat again.
I was so glad, I watched him swallow,
I left the room and let myself smile in the hall,
make a fist, say *Yes*. I should have gone back in
and said thanks for this too, this one more try,
this pain you are going to stretch out longer for
those of us who come and go in the brown chair,
an extra blanket draped across the shoulders
or over the knees. I was grateful, couldn't say it,
walked a victory lap around the ward, went back in
to see if he wanted to stand this morning at the window
and look out.

You Know My Father Prayed for You

You know my father prayed for you—
must have—and for me too.
A quiet man who didn't talk about religion.

The prayers of a man like that.
Perhaps while he poured his raisin bran into a bowl,
while he poured the milk, while he took
a second to look out at the weather.

Perhaps we were there, you and I, in his routine.
What difference does it make, now or ever?
A hawk, winter fog, silent wings.

Most of the time, we take no notice of birds in the air.
It's a red-tail, it's a winter morning on the edge of a city,
a parking lot, a light pole. There is the sound of the cars

on the freeway. Effortless landing, soundless folding
of wings. The prayers of a man like that. A hawk
over snow at the edge of a city.

Lying Up Against My Husband In the Dark

The storm wakes him only enough for two kisses
and a mumble.
The storm: a fine European lady he is not interested in.

Her intermittent temper
her white arms and black taffeta
she's a fine one
she shakes out her dress
oh she's a beauty and she loves him.
Let her pound her fist just above my roof.
I'll keep him in the luxurious dark;
I'll keep the scent of the skin of his back.

She is blips of lightning,
she is hammers, shimmers,
demands commands ultimatums.

Listen: there's a wind in the old broken cedar.

Goodnight fine lady,
I have him in the den
the lair the nest the cave.
The wastrel woman has him,
the nobody lies up against him like a mortal

pretending to have rainy nights to squander,
as if there is no gray hair against the pillow.
The small town girl, the thief,
the neanderthal has him.
Let's yawn,
settle our arms into shadows
under wave after wave on the roof of the cave,
thousands of drops on the shingles,
thousands and thousands on the petals of the oak.

My Old Aunts Play Canasta in a Snowstorm

I ride along in the backseat; the aunt who can drive
picks up each sister at her door, keeps the Pontiac
chugging in each driveway while one or the other
slips into her overshoes and steps out,
closing her door with a click, the wind

lifting the fringe of her white cotton scarf
as she comes down the sidewalk, still pulling on her
new polyester Christmas-stocking mittens.
We have no business to be out in such a storm,
she says, no business at all.

The wind takes her voice and swirls it
like snow across the windshield.
We're on to the next house, the next aunt,
the heater blowing to beat the band.

At the last house, we play canasta,
the deuces wild even as they were in childhood,
the wind blowing through the empty apple trees,
through the shadows of bumper crops. The cards

line up under my aunts' finger bones; eights and nines and aces
straggle and fall into place like well-behaved children.
My aunts shuffle and meld; they laugh like banshees,
as they did in that other kitchen in the 30's—
that day Margaret draped a dishtowel over her face
to answer the door. We put her up to it, they say,
laughing; we pushed her. The man—whoever he was—
drove off in a huff while they laughed 'til they hiccupped,

laughing still—I'm one of the girls laughing him down the sidewalk
and into his car, we're rascals sure as farmyard dogs,
we're wild card-players; the snow thickens,
the coffee boils and perks, the wind is a red trey
because, as one or the other says,

We are getting up there in the years; we'll
have to quit sometime. But today,
today,
deal, sister, deal.